What Black Women Hide For The Sake Of A Black Man's Pride Ultimate Workbook

I'm Done, I can't Take Anymore

Dr. Hallie R. Harper

And

Dr. Jeffery L. Walker

What Black Women Hide For The Sake Of A Black Man's Pride Ultimate Workbook

Also by Dr. Hallie R. Harper

What Black Women Hide For The Sake Of A Black Man's Pride

It's Personal: Looking In and Looking Out

It's Personal: Looking In: Loving Me and Looking Out: Loving You

Reaching Ideal Sisters Embracing Their Finest Women's Empowerment Workbook

RISE: Reaching Ideal Solutions Effectively

It All Starts In The Nest: Why Are You Hurting Each Other?

The Domestic Violence Workbook for African Americans

You Are Chosen To Honor Thyself

African American Females Why Are You So Angry?

A Dream Envisioned: African Americans Struggles and Experiences toward Success in Higher Education in Health Related and Non-Health Related Disciplines

Also by Dr. Jeffery L. Walker

African American Males Why Are You So Angry?

You Are An African American, So Why Are You Talking Like A White Person?

The Prophet

What Black Women Hide For The Sake Of A Black Man's Pride

Perception of African Americans' Use of Linguistic Patterns and the Impact on Attending Higher Education

ACKNOWLEDGEMENT

To all our sisters and brothers who continually struggle with finding peace within themselves to be able to find peace with others!

To those who are unwavering in strength, faith and wisdom we could rely on to challenge and encourage me to always strive for the best!

A special thank you, to Dr. Jeffery Walker, for encouraging me to write this workbook. Giving his input, and challenging me, to tap into the core of every African American woman.

But most of all, we thank God for giving me the power to see a vision to share, challenge, support, encourage, empower, motivate and inspire others!!

DEDICATION

To all who believe and those who want to believe that there is potential and success in all of us!!

AUTHORS POEM

They take my kindness for weakness.

They take my silence for speechless.

They consider my uniqueness strange.

They call my LANGUAGE SLANG.

They see my confidence as conceit.

They see my mistakes as defeat.

They consider my success accidental.

 They minimize my intelligence to "potential."

My questions mean "I'm unaware."

My advancement is somehow unfair.

Any praise is preferential treatment.

To voice concern is contentment.

If I stand up for myself, I'm too defensive.

If I don't trust them, I'm too apprehensive.

I'm defiant if I separate.

I'm fake if I assimilate.

Yet, constantly I am faced with school and workplace hate.

My character is constantly under attack.

Pride for my race makes me, "Too Black."

Yet, I can only be me and, who am I you ask?

 I am a strong African American female/male.

What Black Women Hide For The Sake Of A Black Man's Pride Ultimate Workbook

CONTENTS

What Black Women Hide For The Sake Of A Black Man's Pride Ultimate Workbook

Introduction

"The Ultimate Workbook"

There are many African American women who are sick and tired of being "sick and tired" of the way most African American men treat the African American woman. African American women are starving for someone to step up to the plate and give them direction to understanding the African American man's diabolical ways. African American women are crying aloud for help, unfortunately, no one hears "when dove's cry". African American women are under so much pressure from the African American male, they are walking around in a zombie like state. Those black women who are sick and tired of the bitterness and anger many African American men use as a crutch to cover all of their shortcomings and sins have elected to mate/date a man from another culture. This is so sad but painfully true. Historically African American women are the least likely to date outside their race, however, she almost has no choice because most African American men are a mere shadow of what a real black man used to be. The African American woman practically feels hopeless in her search for a proud, brave, disciplined, kind, strong, intelligent, resourceful, spiritual, and independent man she dreamed she would find. Ladies, there are still a few good men. This workbook is designed to help African American women rise above their environment and take back their God given power to rule as queens to their kings.

The path to success requires cognitive movement (mental agility and awareness) and the ability to understand and accept the reality that you are living under pressure and repeatedly disrespected by the man that you love or think you love.

It is vital, African American women, that you become consistent and persistent when striving to satisfy your emotional appetite. This workbook is the key to unlocking the mystery that has held you in captivity for far too long. It is the way and the light to unraveling the social and emotional web that keeps you in emotional turbulence.......

It is time that you (African American women) step up to the plate and hit a grand slam in terms of experiencing the brighter side of life. The time has come for you to stop blaming others for your own shortcomings, stand up inside of yourself, and say, "**ENOUGH IS ENOUGH**". If you are truly tired, this workbook is your guide to holistic intervention.

Chapter One

Parental Ignorance

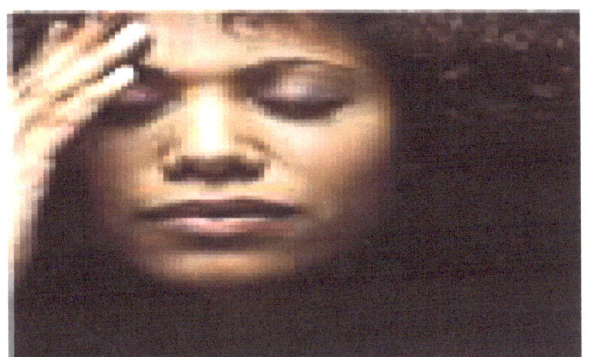

My focus is on the African American mother because she is usually the one who is solitarily raising the male child. Mothers you are to be commended for your incredible efforts in raising a male child in a society where the social pressures are tremendous. When the African American male is absent from the home the male child is robbed of vital instructions.

African American women, why are you so angry? If you are honest with yourself you will concur that it goes back farther than the nest. It stems from the gross negligence and abuse inflicted on you at the hands of your ancestors who endured it from their captures. Yes I'm referring to slavery, but only briefly because I want you to understand how crucial the lessons learned impact your mental, physical, emotional and spiritual wellbeing.

You learned to stuff your true feelings and opinions for fear of being punished or beaten if expressed. You learned to be obedient and submissive for fear of being punished or beaten. But most of all you learned that you were just a mere species placed here for the betterment of others. African American women hear me when I say this, you are not a mere reflection of yourself, and you are beautiful, Nubian queens.

The lessons learned are passed down from generation to generation, no wonder you are angry and don't know why. This form of ignorance can stop with you. You are not chained and bound, you have choices. The greatest injustice you do to yourself is continuing to spread these lessons to your offspring.

African American women be mindful of what you say to others and your children. Be mindful of how you treat yourself and others. Most importantly be mindful of how you allow others to treat you, especially the African American male. This is a damaging message you are sending to your daughter, it is ok to be mistreated and disrespected, and to your son, it is ok to disrespect and mistreat women.

This usually occurs because you didn't spend enough time on the spiritual side to get to know that "perfect black man" before you moved on to the physical side. The only thing that makes sense of such errors in judgment is the fact that most black women are so afraid of being without a man that they accept a man without character. What this entails is that until black women learn to penetrate the exterior and examine the interior of a man they will continue to fall short of finding a "real man." Remember black women that morals, values and your belief system are all internal characteristics that governs your perception towards finding a well balanced black man......"Good Luck!!!"

This chapter was designed to assist you (the reader) in understanding the messages that you received during your developmental stages that ultimately shaped your perception towards "self" the opposite sex, and life in general.

1.   For starters, I define Parental Ignorance as the inability to differentiate between a myth and reality. Many African American mothers are creatures of habit, meaning what was passed down to them; they in return passed that information on to their offspring without forethought. List three important things that you learned from your parent(s) and passed it down to your offspring.

    1._____

    2._____

    3._____

2.   What type of family system did you derive from? Please check the appropriate answer.

        _____ Single parent

_____ Both parents

_____ Grandparent(s)

_____ Uncle

_____ Aunt

_____ Foster parents

3.   In your family system, were the caregiver(s) open for communication or were they more authoritarian(s), meaning that they had an old school ideology, "Do As I Say". Below please elaborate on how your family system communicated with each other.

_____

_____

_____

Most African American children are raised under the "Authoritarian" doctrine and this is not good because it blocks the child from expressing their emotions which can cause internal conflict later in life. This may be one of the causations why many African Americans are so "DAMM" angry.

4.   Now that I have determined what family system you derived from, which category would you say your caregiver(s) represented. Please read the following definitions before you answer this question. An introvert is one who seeks internal pleasure, whereas, an extrovert seeks external pleasure and an ambi-vert has the ability to utilize both. Please put a check mark by the appropriate answer?

_____Introvert

_____Extrovert

_____Ambi-vert

5.   Now! Who in your family system gave you directives (telling you what to do)? Please elaborate:

_____

_____

_____

6.   Were you ever told by your caregiver(s) that you were just like your no good daddy or mother? Please circle the correct answer Yes/No. If yes, please elaborate on what was said.

_____

_____

_____

7.   Did you ever see your mother with another man besides your father when you were growing up? And if so, how did that make you feel? Please elaborate:

_____

_____

_____

8.   During your developmental stages did you ever see your father or another man slap or hit your mother? Yes/No if yes, how did that make you feel? Please elaborate:

_____

_____

_____

9.   Did you ever see your mother crying? If so, did she ever explain to you why she was crying? If so, how did that make you feel? Please elaborate:

_____

_____

_____

10.   Which one of these role models were currently more visual in your community? Please check below.

_____Pimp

_____ Prostitute

_____ Hustler

_____ Rapper

_____ Athlete

_____ Doctor

_____ Nurse

_____ Lawyer

11.   What messages did you receive from the above role models growing up in your home environment? Please elaborate:

_____

_____

_____

12.   During your developmental stages were you angry at your mother or father for not being there for you? If yes, would you elaborate below how that made you feel?

_____

_____

_____

13.   Did you grow up under the welfare system? Yes/No, if yes, how did that make you feel?

_____

_____

_____

14.   Are you currently living under the welfare system with your offspring? Yes/No, if yes, how does this make you feel?

_____

_____

_____

15.   If the father(s) of your offspring(s) is not in the home, is he contributing to the welfare of your child? Yes/No. If yes, please elaborate:

_____

_____

_____

16.   Have you ever:

A) Resented your child because of his/her father? Yes _____ No _____

B) Called your child out of his/her name because of his/her father or for any other reason? Yes ___ No ___

C) Mistreated your child because of his/her father or any other reason?
Yes ___ No ___

D) Ignored your child's needs because of his/her father? Yes ___ No _____

Please elaborate:

_____

_____

_____

The above questions are designed to assist you in looking in retrospect at the messages that you received during your developmental stages. NOW!!!!! Take a second and reflect?

OKAY! Now I am going to get into some sensitive areas. Please remember that your honesty will determine your faith. I am counting on you to make that psychological incision and examine your moral fabric so that you can clear the dust that hinders your vision. Here is where you will begin to understand why you think and behave the way that you do. The first teachers that children will encounter are their parent(s). Children learn to mimic behavior through observation, therefore, a mother/father must be careful what they do and say in front of their offspring. What this entails is that, you (the reader) apparently received messages during your developmental stages that are hindering you today. My aim is to help you modify your perception in a positive way towards "self" and the opposite sex. Remember, that African American men are treating you the way that they are because you are allowing it. **THIS MUST STOP!!!**

17.   During your developmental stages did you ever witness your mother being with different men? Yes/No.? If yes, how did that make you feel? Please elaborate:

_____

_____

_____

18.   In your family system were there multiple fathers, Yes/No. If yes, how many? _____

19.   Do you ever recall hearing your mother having sex? Yes/No. If yes, what messages did you receive and how did that make you feel? Please elaborate:

_____

_____

_____

20.   Did you ever hear your mother say during your developmental stages that all men are dogs, and that all they want is some sex (kitty-cat)? If yes, what were your thoughts? Please elaborate:

_____

_____

_____

21.   Did you grow up hearing that good looking men were better than ugly men? If yes, did you strive to only date good-looking men? Yes/No. Please elaborate:

_____

_____

_____

22.   Have you ever told your girlfriends that you met a fine African American man, but found out that he was no good? Yes/No. If yes, did you become angry and if so, how long did you hold on to it? Please elaborate:

_____

_____

_____

23.   Have you ever forgotten your **morals** (motivation based on ideas of right and wrong), **values** (beliefs which have an emotional investment), and **beliefs** (any thought content held as true) for the sake of a black man's pride?

        Yes/No, if yes, please elaborate:

_____

_____

_____

24.   Because you feared being alone, have you ever accepted a man without **character** (attributes that determines a person's moral, ethical actions and reactions)? Yes/NO, if yes, please elaborate:

_____

_____

_____

25.   Ladies!!!! The first form of attraction is physical, now be honest with yourself, when you first see a man, are you focusing on the way that he looks?

Yes/No, if yes what do looks have to do with personality? Write down the first three things that you look for in a man.

1. _____
2. _____
3. _____

Looking at the below chart rate how important these characteristics are to you. Match your answer with 1-most important; 2- always; 3- usually; 4- sometimes; 5- never; 6- N/A

(In/Ex)Your number 1, if not on list _____   1 2 3 4 5 6

(In/Ex) Your number 2, if not on list _____   1 2 3 4 5 6

(In/Ex) Your number 3, if not on list _____   1 2 3 4 5 6

(Ex) Facial Looks (fine brother)   1 2 3 4 5 6

(Ex) Physically Fit (six pack abs)   1 2 3 4 5 6

(Ex)Well Dressed   1 2 3 4 5 6

(In) Sense of Humor   1 2 3 4 5 6

(In) Intellectual   1 2 3 4 5 6

(In)Smells Good   1 2 3 4 5 6

When looking over your choices, how important are the internal/external characteristics to you? This will help you see why you keep making the decisions you do when seeking a mate, Please elaborate:

_____
_____
_____

What did you discover? I **do/don't** make decisions based on what is in my best interest? Yes/No, Please elaborate:

_____

_____

_____

_____

Now go back and reflect on this chapter, and you will find that 90% of your problems with African American men are because of your inability to penetrate the exterior of a man and examine the interior of a man, which is where you will find substance.

Self-Awareness Chart: Rate yourself from 1-5 on how often you are aware of the following.

Day of the Week: _____

Today, I worked on overcoming challenges in my life.　　　　*1 2 3 4 5*

Today, I made decisions based on what was best for me.　　　　*1 2 3 4 5*

Today, I focused on my strengths to stay encouraged and motivated.　*1 2 3 4 5*

Today, I was able to stay calm and relaxed when things happened in my life.

1 2 3 4 5

Today, I practiced saying I'm ok just as I am, and right now this is enough for me.

1 2 3 4 5

1-5 = Ouch, you are not in touch with who you are. The good news is that you have an opportunity to improve the way that you view yourself.

6-10=   You still need a lot of work to discover who you are.

11-15 = You are half way there keep working. You are good at some aspects of self-awareness, but there's room for improvements.

16-20 = You are becoming more aware of who you are or destined to become.

21-25 = You are in touch with who you are.

Chapter Two

What Black Men want Black Women to know about Black Men

How many times have you said to yourself, "I love him but I don't understand him?" Do you recall saying, "I have given him everything and he still is unhappy?" It is almost like no matter what you do for him he still treats you like bowel movement. Does this ring a bell for you? If so, then this workbook is 99.9 percent accurate. This might explain why black women endure so much pain from black men and continue to choose black men who are **dead in the head**.

Black women-wake up and smell the coffee!!! What is it going to take before you start to love yourself first? When are you going to stop inflicting pain upon yourself? Yes! A lot of your internal conflict is self-inflicted because the black man is not sharp and because the black woman continues to be naïve and defunct in her thinking. Stop blaming the black man for your own shortcomings and stand-up inside of yourselves and rise. No offense ladies, but it is what it is. Stop it now before you become a biological or psychological statistic!!! This means that he kills you, you kill yourself or you allow him to drive you into total darkness (insanity).

I want you black women to know that many black men are not dogs. That is an understatement. They are **social predators** that prey on the weak so that they can get all of their needs met (money and having multiple sex partners). Black women you need to know that you allow it!!! Remember black women, what makes a predator sharp is ignorance on your behalf. So black women when you allow yourself to be used by him he will continue to see you as an object and this is not good for you.

Black women, black men don't respect themselves so how can you expect for them to respect you. It really is not that difficult to figure out. Black women stop giving these black men power to misuse you.

This chapter was designed to assist you (the reader) in understanding the messages that you received from black men that ultimately shaped your perception towards "self" the opposite sex, and life in general.

1.   When you say "I love you" to your man, and turn around and say, "I don't understand him" Do you know what love is? Yes/No, Please elaborate: Do you understand the internal/external, verbal/non-verbal communications he directly or indirectly gives you? Yes/No, How does this make you feel? Please elaborate:

_____

_____

_____

2.   Looking back, particularly to the early 1970's, during this era there was a movie released titled "Super Fly", in which the image of a pimp/hustler was supposedly personified of a ladies' man. It displayed women as objects with little or no respect. Have you ever been treated as an object by your man? Yes/No, if yes, why did you allow it? How did this make you feel? Please elaborate:

_____

_____

_____

3.   Have you ever been put in a position by your man that it was your responsibility to support him in any way he wants, knowing it was wrong? Yes/No, if yes, how did this make you feel? Are you in this situation now? Yes/No, if yes, please elaborate:

_____

_____

_____

4.   Have you ever surrendered your individuality and allowed yourself to be treated poorly and accepted cruel and unusual punishment from your man? Yes/No, if yes, why did you do it? How did this make you feel? Please elaborate:

_____

_____

_____

5.   Have you ever used alcohol and drugs to please your man? Yes/No, if yes how did this make you feel? Were you ever forced to use alcohol or drugs by your man? Yes/No, if yes, how did this make you feel? Please elaborate:

_____

_____

_____

6.   Have you ever been called a b_____ or whore by your man? Yes/No, if yes how did this make you feel? Do you allow and accept this as common communications between you and your man? Yes/No, if yes please elaborate:

_____

_____

_____

7.   When asked the definition of Love, you will get many different definitions. What is your definition for "Self-Love"? Please list 3 things that you believe define self-love?

1) _____

2) _____

3) _____

8.   Have you ever been in a relationship and knew that you were sharing your man with another woman? Yes/No, if yes, why did you do it? How did this make you feel? If you are still in the relationship, why? And did you know any of the other women he was sleeping with? Yes/No, if yes how did this make you feel? Please elaborate:

_____

_____

_____

Alright my beautiful Black Nubian queens, I am going to give you some valuable insight on how to determine a **"Predictor"** from a **"Predator,"** which is both **"Dead In The Head".** First of all, in case you didn't know this ladies, the dating game sets you up for failure because human beings, specifically, most African American males are not what they appear to be on the on-sight of meeting them. Although, Black men would straight-up deny this because it is a direct blow to the Black man's ego and pseudo pride. However, I am clearly going to define the two terms because I want you beautiful Black ladies to be able to differentiate between these two diabolical creatures, and I mean that literally. Remember ladies that the **"Social Predictor"** is very good-looking and extremely suave with a smooth tongue. He dresses nice and smells wonderful with the ability to articulate to your desire. The **"Social Predictor"** will use strategic and methodical moves to create an illusion to manipulate your desire for him. Matter of fact, he will use what we call the **"God Father Theory"** he will set you up and put you in a position where you cannot refuse him, by simply being overly kind to you. Remember ladies, there is no defense for kindness, and he has mastered the art of manipulation. On the other hand, the **"Social Predator"** is ghetto because he has an anti-social personality. His primary goal is to get what he can from you and put his tennis shoes on and run, leaving you emotionally paralyzed. He is unable to feel any remorse and he is only concerned about getting his needs met--------Do you know anyone like this?

I am going to ask you a series of questions to determine if you have been a victim of either one of these **"Social Predictors or Predators".**

9.   When his external is shinning more than his internal, what messages did you receive from this? Please elaborate below.

_____

_____

_____

10.   Does your man lack intestinal fortitude (drive and will power)? Yes/No, if yes, are you still with him? Yes/No, if yes, why? Please elaborate below.

_____

_____

_____

11.   When your man is not at work, does he spend a lot of time with his buddies? Yes/No, if yes, how does that make you feel? Please elaborate below?

_____

_____

_____

12.   When he goes out to nightclubs with his buddies, do you trust him? Yes/No, if no, how does that make you feel, and why are you still with him? Please elaborate below?

_____

_____

_____

13.   Have you ever noticed that sometimes when your man comes in from a night out with his buddies, he is not in the mood for sex? Did you ever question his behavior? Yes/No, if yes, what was his response? Please elaborate below?

_____

_____

_____

14.   Have you ever notice your man changing his wardrobe (becoming more fashionable)? Yes/No, if yes, did you question it? Yes/No, if yes, what were your thoughts? Please elaborate below?

_____

_____

_____

15.   Have you ever paid close attention to your man's body scent? If so, have you ever noticed that when he returns from being away from the home he smells different? Yes/No, if yes, did you become suspicious Yes/No and if yes, how did you confront him? Please elaborate below if applicable?

_____

_____

_____

16.   Have you ever notice that your man all of a sudden has trouble maintaining eye-contact? Yes/No, if yes, did you talk to him about why he can't look at you? If yes, how did you respond to his answer? Please elaborate below?

_____

_____

_____

17.   Do you have the type of man that tries to control you by saying what you can and cannot do? Yes/No, if yes, please elaborate below how that makes you feel?

_____

_____

_____

18.   Have you ever noticed that when your girlfriends are visiting you, you noticed that your man is starring at one of them, especially if she is attractive and curvaceous (shapely)? Yes/No, if yes, what did you do about it and how did this situation make you feel. Please elaborate below?

_____

_____

_____

The above characteristics will give you some insight on how to pay closer attention to some major characteristics that Black men think that they are hiding from you.

Self-Awareness Chart: Rate yourself from 1-5 on how often you are aware of the following.

Day of the Week: _____

Today, I worked on overcoming challenges in my life.   *1 2 3 4 5*

Today, I made decisions based on what was best for me.   *1 2 3 4 5*

Today, I focused on my strengths to stay encouraged and motivated.   *1 2 3 4 5*

Today, I was able to stay calm and relaxed when things happened in my life.

1 2 3 4 5

Today, I practiced saying I'm ok just as I am, and right now this is enough for me.

1 2 3 4 5

_____

1-5 = Ouch, you are not in touch with who you are. The good news is that you have an opportunity to improve the way that you view yourself.

6-10=   You still need a lot of work to discover who you are.

11-15 = You are half way there keep working. You are good at some aspects of self-awareness, but there's room for improvements.

16-20 = You are becoming more aware of who you are or destined to become.

21-25 = You are in touch with who you are.

Chapter Three

What Black Women want Black men to know about Black Women

I have discovered that black women all have one thing in common ----We are tired of black men misunderstanding, misjudging and mistreating black women. My black Nubian queens, take back your power. It is true that the black men and women were born into royalty, you are kings and queens. It saddens me to see that throughout history, you have forgotten this very important and substantial reality, not fictional but a fact.

Instead of living and treating each other as such, black women you are allowing the black man to treat you as slaves, programmed to meet their every need. You complain "I'm not his maid", but yet you don't stand up and demand to be treated as you rightfully deserve. My sisters, have you made your wants, needs and desires clear? Do you carry yourself with respect, but allow the black man to treat you with disrespect? If you are honest with yourself the black man will treat you just the way you allow him to. The black woman is the anchor in both the biblical and humanistic paradigm of the black man's development.

Black men are creatures of habit and will often say one thing and do another. And they say black women are confusing and complicated!

I believe, if we could stop blaming each other and start listening to each other, black men would see that black women have the capability of loving them in a way no other race can or will.

This chapter was designed to assist you (the reader) in understanding the messages that you send black men that ultimately shaped your perception towards "self" the opposite sex, and life in general.

1.	How many times have you said to yourself, you wish your man knew what you wanted? _____. Have you ever told your man what you wanted? Yes/No, have you ever asked him for clarification about if he understood your wants? Yes/No, please elaborate:

_____

_____

_____

2.   Has your man ever said to you "I know you and what you need" meaning he feels he knows you better than you know yourself conversation? Yes/No, if yes what did you do or say? How did this make you feel? Please elaborate:

_____

_____

_____

3.   Which of these characteristics were you told by your man that you have?

Possessiveness _____

Bossy _____

Status seeking _____

Picky _____

Selective _____

Please name 3 characteristics you feel describes you:

1) _____
2) _____
3) _____

4.   You all want men you can respect and appreciate, do you respect and appreciate your man? Yes/No, if not, why are you still with him? Please elaborate:

_____

_____

_____

5.   Have you ever dated a man who is unemployed and uneducated? Yes/No if yes, how did you feel? Do you still date him? Yes/No, if yes, please elaborate:

_____

_____

_____

6.   If single, do you have to defend your single status in every social situation imaginable? Yes/No, if yes, why do you do it and how does this make you feel? Do you feel that the black men are intimidated by you and avoiding you? Yes/No, if yes please elaborate:

_____

_____

_____

7.   Have you ever felt guilty for being educated and making more money than your man? Yes/No, if yes, please elaborate:

_____

_____

_____

8.   Have you ever been labeled stuck-up or difficult by the black man? Yes/No, by your man? Yes/No, if yes, how did this make you feel and how did you handle the situation? Please elaborate:

_____

_____

_____

9.   Ladies, please rate the specific qualities you desire in the black man according to the level of importance to you, 10 – being the most important and 1 – being the least important.

He needs to be externally and internally attractive _____

He needs to be spiritually sound, guided and maintain social balance _____

He needs to have obtained some level of education beyond high school _____

He needs to be humble and clean _____

He needs to be disease free _____

He needs to be drug free _____

He needs to be able to admit when he is wrong _____

He needs to be creative _____

He needs to be romantic holistically _____

He needs to be my friend _____

After looking at this chart, how many of the above qualities does your man have? Please elaborate:

_____
_____
_____

10.   Have you ever been treated like a bank: quick deposit with immediate withdrawals? Yes/No, if yes, why do you allow it and how does this make you feel? Please elaborate:

_____
_____
_____

11.   Have you ever been treated like a fitness center: sex without emotion (workout)? Yes/No, if yes, why do you allow it and how does this make you feel? Please elaborate:

_____
_____
_____

12.   Have you ever been treated like a restaurant: personal chef and short order cook? Yes/No, if yes, why do you allow it and how does this make you feel? Please elaborate:

_____
_____
_____

13.   Ladies, does your man spend quality time with you? Yes/No, if no, what do you do about it? How does it make you feel? Why are you still with him? Please elaborate:

_____
_____
_____

14.   Ladies, does your man spend more time at work than with you? Yes/No, if yes, what do you do about it? How does it make you feel? Why are you still with him? Please elaborate:

_____
_____
_____

15.   Ladies, does your man spend more time with the boys than with you? Yes/No, if yes, what do you do about it? How does it make you feel? Why are you still with him? Please elaborate:

_____
_____
_____

16.   How many times has a black man said he was going to call you and didn't? _____ how did this make you feel? Please elaborate:

_____

_____

_____

17.   Ladies, does your man treat you like his maid instead of his woman? Yes/No, if yes, what do you do about it? How does it make you feel? Why are you still with him? Please elaborate:

_____

_____

_____

18.   Ladies, does your man send you flowers, cards, a text message and smiles/laughs with you instead of at you showing he cares? Yes/No, if no, what do you do about it? How does it make you feel? Why are you still with him? Please elaborate:

_____

_____

_____

19.   Ladies, does your man support your dreams, goals, and career? Yes/No, if no, what do you do about it? How does it make you feel? Why are you still with him? Please elaborate:

_____

_____

_____

20.   Ladies, have you ever been cheated on, lied to and most of all taken for granted by your man? Yes/No, if yes, what do you do about it? How does it make you feel? Why are you still with him? Please elaborate:

_____

_____

_____

21.   Ladies, do you have open and honest communications with your man, does he really talk and listen to you? Yes/No, if no, what do you do about it? How does it make you feel? Why are you still with him? Please elaborate:

_____

_____

_____

22.   How important is the amount of money a man makes if honesty, integrity, communications, love, intimacy, passion and romance were not present? Please elaborate:

_____

_____

_____

23.   When it comes to interracial dating, do you have a problem with black men dating outside their race? Yes/No, if yes, please elaborate:

_____

_____

_____

24.   Would you date a man of another race? Yes/No, have you ever dated a man of another race? Yes/No, please elaborate:

_____

_____

_____

25.   Not all women are seeking a husband with every man she meets, however, would you admit to yourself that you want a commitment someday? Yes/No, if no, please elaborate:

_____

_____

_____

26.   My sisters, I know this question is very serious and sensitive, however bare with me. Have you ever been in or are in an emotionally _____, sexually ____, spiritually ____, physically ____ abusive relationship? Yes/No, if yes what are you doing about it? How does it make you feel? And why are you still with him? Please elaborate:

_____

_____

_____

The pain and hurt you have been inflicted with whether intentional or unintentional is real and may go away with time, but the memory does not. It is often healthy to remember the hurt to prevent it from happening again.

This chapter highlighted the important things black women need black men to know and understand about them. The goal for this chapter was not only to assist black women with valuable insight into how they are actually being treated by the black man, but to give them a voice and avenue in which to be heard and assess if their needs and wants are being met.

Self-Awareness Chart: Rate yourself from 1-5 on how often you are aware of the following.

Day of the Week: _____

Today, I worked on overcoming challenges in my life.   *1 2 3 4 5*

Today, I made decisions based on what was best for me.   *1 2 3 4 5*

Today, I focused on my strengths to stay encouraged and motivated.   *1 2 3 4 5*

Today, I was able to stay calm and relaxed when things happened in my life.

1 2 3 4 5

Today, I practiced saying I'm ok just as I am, and right now this is enough for me.

1 2 3 4 5

_____

1-5 = Ouch, you are not in touch with who you are. The good news is that you have an opportunity to improve the way that you view yourself.

6-10=   You still need a lot of work to discover who you are.

11-15 = You are half way there keep working. You are good at some aspects of self-awareness, but there's room for improvements.

16-20 = You are becoming more aware of who you are or destined to become.

21-25 = You are in touch with who you are.

Chapter Four

Human Sexuality

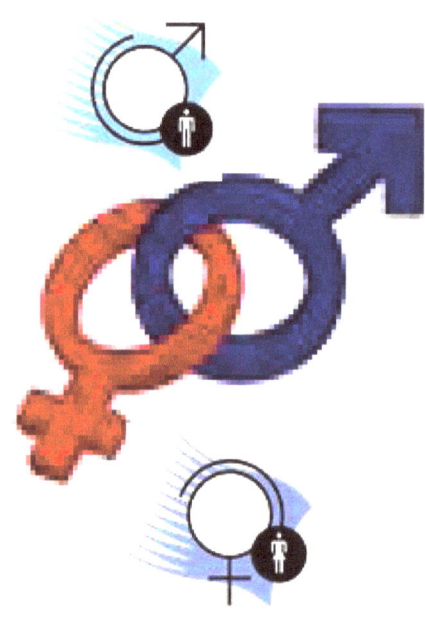

This chapter is extremely important because many African American males and females are unaware of the fact, that **"Human Sexuality"** is the crazy glue that holds relationships together. According to vital statistics, the divorce rates for African Americans are **"Off The Chain"** and more and more African American women are having extra-marital affairs because they are tired of being sexually mistreated by African American males. One of the reasons why African Americans are not relating to each other is because they don't understand the significance of **"Human Touch".** It is safe to assume, that most African Americans allow myths and fallacies to govern their perception towards **"Human Sexuality".**

First of all, most African American males lack intellectual substance towards human sexuality because they think that they know all that they need to know about sex-----right? Wrong. Did you know that most African American women go through life without ever reaching a true orgasm? Instead, they reach what is known as an **"Orgasmic Spasm"**. Matter of fact, they lie to their mate about reaching an orgasm because they don't want to deflate his pseudo ego.......Ladies you know that I'm right on the money, so stand up and get real with this, because if you don't, you will continue to live a life that is unfulfilled.

Ladies!!! You need to understand, that African American males receive mixed messages during their development stages towards **"Human Sexuality".** Black men honestly believe that they are **"All That"** when it comes to making holistic love to their mate. The bottom line is, most Black men don't even know what holistic love is, so how can they be **"All That"** but, perhaps they could be, if they would allow themselves to become sexually intelligent. And, one of the ways that they can become sexually intelligent is by sitting down with their mate and asking the female what does she like and how do she like it. At this point, all he has to do is humble himself and do exactly what she says and he cannot go wrong-----right ladies?

In this section, you will discover that you have allowed the African American male to misuse you sexually by being unaware. My hope is to enhance your awareness towards your own sexuality and come to terms with the fact, that you are the **"Gold"** and that all men are prospectors-----do you remember reading in the book about the definition of a prospector. In case you have forgotten, a prospector is one who searches for **"GOLD"** do you get it now----- you are the **"GOLD"**.

Here, you will be asked a series of questions to determine your sexual awareness towards the African American male. Keep in mind, that your honesty will enable you to rise above your ignorance and help you to determine a **"Social Predictor from a Social Predator"**.

1.   Was human sexuality ever discussed in your family setting during your developmental stages? Yes/No, if yes, what was discussed? Please elaborate below?

_____
_____
_____

2.   Are you comfortable with your sexuality? Yes/No, if no, please elaborate:

_____
_____
_____

3.   At what age did you lose your virginity? _____

4.   Was your first sexual experience what you expected? Yes/No, if no, please elaborate:

_____
_____
_____

5.   How many offspring do you have? _____ If more than one, do they have the same father? Yes/No. If no, please elaborate below?

_____
_____
_____

6.   Have you ever experienced intimacy (in-to-me-see) from your man? Yes/No, if no, please elaborate:

_____
_____
_____

7.   Ladies, in your opinion do intimacy come before sex or after sex? Please elaborate:

_____
_____
_____

8.   Ladies, there exist two forms of connecting one individual to another, first, there is sex- consisting of the mount, thrush and crash, in which your man rolls over and goes to sleep. Second, there is lovemaking- consisting of kissing, fondling, deep breathing and tender exchange of verbal communications. Which form of intimacy are you currently experiencing with your man? Sex _____ Lovemaking _____Are you satisfied? Yes/No, if no, what are you doing about it? Please elaborate:

_____
_____
_____

9.   When you are intimate with your man, are you getting what you need and want from him? Yes/No, if yes congratulations, if no, what are you doing about it? Please elaborate:

_____
_____
_____

10.   Have you ever faked an orgasm? Yes/No, if yes was it often, seldom and how did you feel afterwards? Please elaborate:

_____

_____

11.   Have you ever engaged in oral sex? Yes/No, have you ever engaged in anal sex? Yes/No

12. Are you open to experiencing new things with your man? Yes/No, if not, why are you still with him? Please elaborate:

_____

_____

13.   When you are intimate with your man, does he mentally stimulate you? Yes/No, if not what are you doing about it? Please elaborate:

_____

_____

14.   Have you ever had a conversation with your man and he asked you what you liked and disliked during sex? Yes/No, if not how does this make you feel? Please elaborate:

_____

_____

15.   Have you ever used sex to get what you wanted? Yes/No, if yes how did this make you feel? Please elaborate:

_____

_____

16.   Have you ever had unprotected sex because the man refused to wear protection? Yes/No, if yes, how did this make you feel? Please elaborate:

_____
_____
_____

17.   Have you ever been in a relationship strictly for convenience? Yes/No, if yes, are you getting what you want? Yes/No, if not, why are you still with him? Please elaborate:

_____
_____
_____

18.   Have you ever been in a relationship with one man, but in love with another? Yes/No, if yes, why are you still in the relationship? Please elaborate:

_____
_____
_____

19.   Have you ever been in a relationship in which your man told you he was in love with another woman? Yes/No, if yes, how does this make you feel? And why are you still with him? Please elaborate:

_____
_____
_____

20.   Have you ever had sex just to release? Yes/No

21.   Have you ever been in love with someone who was committed/married to someone else? Yes/No, if yes how did this make you feel and what did you do about it? Please elaborate:

_____
_____
_____

22.   Have you ever dated a married man? Yes/No, if yes, how did this make you feel? If still involved what are you thinking? (It won't work) please elaborate:

_____
_____
_____

22.   Have you ever had a fantasy to have sex with more than one partner at a time? Yes/No

23.   Do you feel like you are settling for less than you desire in a man? Yes/No, if yes, what do you plan to do about it? Please elaborate:

_____
_____
_____

24.   When you are intimate with your man are you more focused on the number of times you can please him or the quality of your intimacy? Please elaborate:

_____
_____
_____

25.   Are you and your man equally yoked or connected spiritually? Yes/No, if not, how does this make you feel and what are you doing about it? Please elaborate:

_____
_____
_____

Ladies, it has been my intention to assist you in becoming more aware of your own sexuality, needs, wants and desires. If any question made you feel uncomfortable, please take some time to reflect on and examine why you are experiencing emotional turbulence, so you can alleviate the internal conflict you are experiencing.

Self-Awareness Chart: Rate yourself from 1-5 on how often you are aware of the following.

Day of the Week: _____

Today, I worked on overcoming challenges in my life.   1 2 3 4 5

Today, I made decisions based on what was best for me.   1 2 3 4 5

Today, I focused on my strengths to stay encouraged and motivated.   1 2 3 4 5

Today, I was able to stay calm and relaxed when things happened in my life.

1 2 3 4 5

Today, I practiced saying I'm ok just as I am, and right now this is enough for me.

1 2 3 4 5

1-5 = Ouch, you are not in touch with who you are. The good news is that you have an opportunity to improve the way that you view yourself.

6-10= You still need a lot of work to discover who you are.

11-15 = You are half way there keep working. You are good at some aspects of self-awareness, but there's room for improvements.

16-20 = You are becoming more aware of who you are or destined to become.

21-25 = You are in touch with who you are.

Chapter Five

Economic deprivation

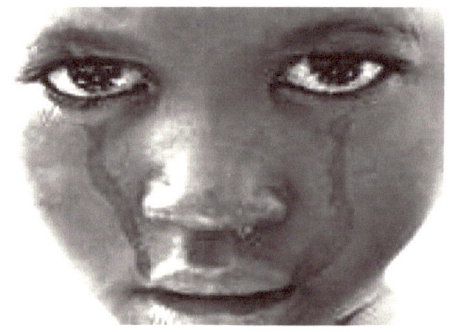

Money is necessary to barter in the United States system and without it, **"you are through dancing".** So why African American women, are you choosing men who are allergic to money, in terms of working for it in the right way? It appears that many African American women are gravitating towards men who are in the fast lane because they display fancy cars, clothes and a roll of paper bills----is that all that you are looking for? If so, I feel very sorry for you because you suffer from a severe form of psychological cataracts, meaning you cannot see clearly.

Economic deprivation is a term used to describe an individual who lacks that **'giddy-up"** to prepare themselves to combat the financial ills that society will most definitely hit you with. Motivational speaker, Les Brown states, that life sometimes will knock you down and when it does hopefully you will land on your back because if "you can look up, you can get up". What this entails is that, it is **"better to be prepared and have an opportunity, than to have an opportunity and not be prepared".** But, for some strange reason many African American women do not understand this powerful concept......Why is this? Could it be that you African American women suffer from the "Pleasure Principle," meaning that you are attracted to glitter? Is it possible that you beautiful ladies have trouble differentiating between "instant and delayed gratification"? **Listen sweethearts,** instant gratification lacks substance, where delayed gratification enhances substance------and you can only find substance on the spiritual side of a human being..........Don't get it twisted?

Many African American females across the United States are having sex according to pleasure and not their income, and who suffers in the long-run? The offspring but you don't think about that during the heat of passion-----do you? Don't you Black women realize that we are at **"zero population"** meaning, most African American women are having multiple children without having the financial means to accurately support them, and you want to know why our children are terribly distorted today? They are angry because they grew up in a family system that was not **"poor'**, but **"broke"** because the mother did not set the stage before her child arrived. I focus on mothers because I already know that many African American fathers are **"dead in the head"** and he is nowhere to be found with his coward self------right? This doesn't necessarily mean that all

African American males are negligent, but for the most part, many African American males run from their biological responsibilities and are living under the floorboard of society so that they don't have to stand up and be a **"Real Man"** and there is a reason why they are the way that they are.

They are duplicating a behavior that was passed down to them through what I call "Genetic transfusion." ladies; you know that I'm right? Keep in mind, that statistics supports my observation.

Thus far, I believe that I have clearly demonstrated that part of the blame lies on your shoulders (African American women) meaning, that once you become holistically savvy, you will be able to differentiate between a "social predictor and a social predator). Herein, lies hope that you will accept this revelation that hopefully will clear the dust that has hindered your vision.

1.   Do you look for a man to take care of you? Yes/No. If yes, Please elaborate:

_____
_____
_____

2.   Before you have sex with a man do you think about his financial and character status? Yes/No.

3.   Are you conscious of the fact, that having sex is the equation of pregnancy? Yes/No. If yes, did you think about if he could financially support the offspring? Yes/No. Please elaborate:

_____
_____
_____

4.   After your first child, did he accommodate you in supporting this child? Yes/No. If no, are you still with him? if yes, why? Please elaborate:

_____
_____
_____

Write a letter in full detail explaining why you allowed the African American male to keep you in total captivity.

_____
_____
_____
_____
_____
_____
_____
_____
_____
_____
_____
_____
_____
_____
_____
_____
_____
_____
_____
_____
_____
_____
_____
_____
_____
_____
_____
_____
_____
_____
_____
_____

Self-Awareness Chart: Rate yourself from 1-5 on how often you are aware of the following.

Day of the Week: _____

Today, I worked on overcoming challenges in my life.   *1 2 3 4 5*

Today, I made decisions based on what was best for me.   *1 2 3 4 5*

Today, I focused on my strengths to stay encouraged and motivated.   *1 2 3 4 5*

Today, I was able to stay calm and relaxed when things happened in my life.

1 2 3 4 5

Today, I practiced saying I'm ok just as I am, and right now this is enough for me.

1 2 3 4 5

1-5 = Ouch, you are not in touch with who you are. The good news is that you have an opportunity to improve the way that you view yourself.

6-10= You still need a lot of work to discover who you are.

11-15 = You are half way there keep working. You are good at some aspects of self-awareness, but there's room for improvements.

16-20 = You are becoming more aware of who you are or destined to become.

21-25 = You are in touch with who you are.

FINAL CALL

My beautiful sisters, it has been a privilege and honor to write this insightful workbook. It is my hope that you will keep an open mind and willing ear to see, hear and receive what awaits you upon unveiling the real you.

As you reflect on your answers remember that you are **"Queens"** take back your power and throne. And finally when and if you start to stumble, fall or doubt yourself recite the following:

"I'm through Hiding for the Sake of a Black Man's Pride"

I'm through hiding for the sake of a black man's pride

What I really feel

I'm through hiding for the sake of a black man's pride

It's time to be real

I'm through hiding for the sake of a black man's pride

What I need

I'm through hiding for the sake of a black man's pride

My God, I have a soul to feed

I'm through hiding for the sake of a black man's pride

What I desire

I'm through hiding for the sake of a black man's pride

Listen up, my brothers, I'll tell you what I require

I'm through hiding for the sake of a black man's pride

-Dr. Hallie R. Harper-

RISE

The RISE model used in connection with the Self-Awareness Chart, is helpful in understanding your options which assist you in maintaining your balance when dealing with your man.

R-Reflect & Examine: this step provides you with a starting point to begin thinking about your situation and allows you opportunities to examine the options available toward understanding them.

I-Imagine & Intentions: this step encourages you to tap into your imagination to create a vision to assist in developing realistic options and plans to accomplish them.

S-Solutions: this step will assist you to continue to explore in detail the options you listed and the advantages of each one.

E-Evaluate: this step helps you determine if your solutions are realistic and obtainable, if so select an option or options.

NOW RISE! IF YOU CAN LOOK UP, YOU CAN GET UP!!!!

RISE Model

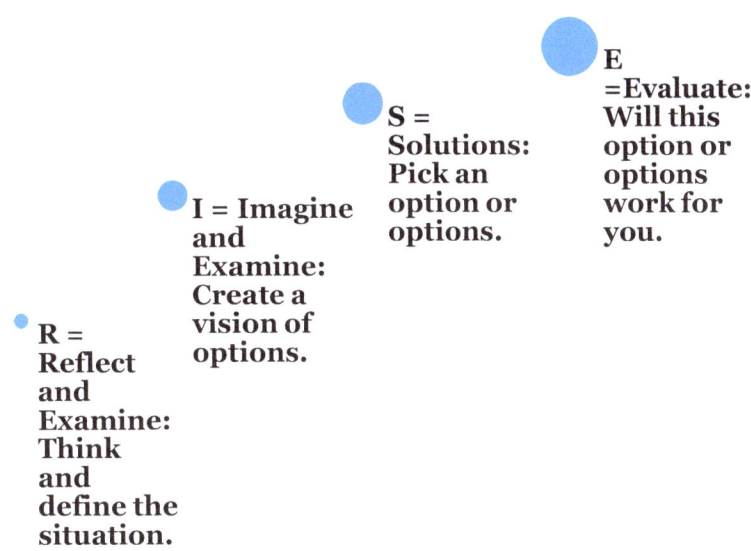

E =Evaluate: Will this option or options work for you.

S = Solutions: Pick an option or options.

I = Imagine and Examine: Create a vision of options.

R = Reflect and Examine: Think and define the situation.

Reviewing Your Options

One of the primary reasons for using the RISE model is to assist in reaching solutions to any situation you encounter. This can be accomplished by using the RISE Model on a daily basis.

What is the situation I'm dealing with?

_____
_____
_____

What can I do about this situation?

_____
_____
_____

What did I do about this situation?

_____

_____

_____

Did this solution work for me?

_____

_____

_____

Self-Awareness Chart: Rate yourself from 1-5 on how often you are aware of the following.

Day of the Week: _____

Today, I worked on overcoming challenges in my life.　　　*1 2 3 4 5*

Today, I made decisions based on what was best for me.　　*1 2 3 4 5*

Today, I focused on my strengths to stay encouraged and motivated.　*1 2 3 4 5*

Today, I was able to stay calm and relaxed when things happened in my life.

1 2 3 4 5

Today, I practiced saying I'm ok just as I am, and right now this is enough for me.

1 2 3 4 5

1-5 = Ouch, you are not in touch with who you are. The good news is that you have an opportunity to improve the way that you view yourself.

6-10= You still need a lot of work to discover who you are.

11-15 = You are half way there keep working. You are good at some aspects of self-awareness, but there's room for improvements.

16-20 = You are becoming more aware of who you are or destined to become.

21-25 = You are in touch with who you are.

AUTHORS SPECIAL POAMS

YOU ARE A WOMAN

You are a woman who knows it is right and good you are a woman. A woman who honors your experience and tells your stories.

You are a woman who knows you are good. A woman who trusts and respects yourself. Who listens to your needs and desires and meets them with tenderness and grace.

You are a woman who has acknowledged the past's influence on the present. A woman who has walked through your past. Who has healed into the present.

You are a woman who authors your own life. A woman, who exerts, initiates and moves on your own behalf. Who refuses to surrender except to your truest self and your wisest voice.

You are a woman in love with your own body. A woman who knows her body is enough, just as it is. Who celebrates your body and its rhythms and cycles as an exquisite resource.

You are a woman who celebrates the accumulation of your years and your wisdom. Who refuses to use precious energy disguising the changes in your body and life.

You are a woman who values the women in your life. A woman, who sits in circles of women. Who is reminded of the truth about yourself when you forgets.

- Patricia Lynn Reilly -

"IT'S UP TO YOU"

GOD gave you this day to do just what you would.

YOU can throw it away or do something good.

YOU can make someone happy, or make someone sad.

WHAT have you done with the day that you had?

GOD gave it to you to do just as you would.

YOU can do what is wicked or do something good.

YOU can hand out a smile or give'em a frown.

YOU can lift someone up, or push someone down.

YOU can lighten a load or some progress impede.

YOU can look for a rose or just gather some weed.

WHAT did you do with your BEAUTIFUL day?

GOD gave it to you did you throw it away?

~Unknown Author~

Ladies I have given you vital instruction, it's now up to you!!!!

Remember the same things that make you laugh can make you cry!!!!

References

Giclee Print (2010). African American woman and six children at window of a city apartment building-1950. Retrieved June 12, from www.allposters.com

Microsoft Office Professional. *(2007). Microsoft Office Online ClipArt/Bing selected images and graphics*. Redmond, WA: Microsoft Corporation One Microsoft Way

Miller, D. (2003). *Your Surviving Spirit: A Spiritual Workbook For Coping With Trauma*. Oakland: New Harbinger Publications, Inc.

Norment, L. (1997). Sex and sisters: what turns women on and off? Ebony, 5, v52

Norment, L. (1992). What Black women really want in a man Ebony, 5, v47?

Randolph, L.B. (1991). Secrets about Black woman every Black man should know – Turn-ons and turn-offs in relationships – Cover Story. Ebony, 9, v46

Swagger, Mr. (2009). Why Are Successful Black Woman Single? A Black Man's Perspective. Fresh Express, from www.swagger.com

Stanton, C. (2006). Life Coach in a Box. *Life Coach in a Box* . San Francisco, CA, USA: Chronical Books.

Viscott, D. (1974). How To Live with Another Person. New York: Arbor House.

Personal Touch & Care Enterprise Inc. (RISE)

What Black Women Hide for the Sake of a Black Man's Pride

The Ultimate Workbook Feedback Sheet

Please circle the appropriate answer

1. I participated actively and contributed thoughtfully throughout this workbook. Yes/No

2. The workbook promoted self-directed learning, including reflection and self-assessment. Yes/No

3. The workbook increased my desire to continue learning more about issues affecting African American males and females. Yes/No

4. The authors encouraged me to connect my lived experiences with the information received from this workbook. Yes/No

5. The authors communicated ideas and information clearly and effectively. Yes/No

6. The authors provided several opportunities for participation to learn from each question. Yes/No

7. Would you recommend this workbook to someone else? Yes/No

8. What specific changes would you recommend to enhance the transfer of

learning?

_____

_____

_____

_____

Send completed form to:
Dr. Harper or Dr. Walker
5635 Kansas Avenue
Suite 225
Omaha, NE 68104-1226

THANK YOU FOR YOUR PARTICIPATION!!!

www.ingramcontent.com/pod-product-compliance
Lightning Source LLC
Chambersburg PA
CBHW041505280526
45792CB00004B/1133